DATE DUE

DEMCO 38-296

WEATHER AND CLIMATE

DISCARD

Please visit our web site at: **www.garethstevens.com**
**For a free color catalog describing Gareth Stevens Publishing's list of
high-quality books and multimedia programs, call 1-800-542-2595 (USA)
or 1-800-387-3178 (Canada). Gareth Stevens Publishing's fax: (414) 332-3567.**

Library of Congress Cataloging-in-Publication Data available upon request from
publisher. Fax (414) 336-0157 for the attention of the Publishing Records Department.

ISBN 0-8368-3386-4

This edition first published in 2004 by
Gareth Stevens Publishing
A World Almanac Education Group Company
330 West Olive Street, Suite 100
Milwaukee, WI 53212 USA

This U.S. edition copyright © 2004 by Gareth Stevens, Inc. First published in
1999 as *Boom: The Weather & Climate Files* by Discovery Enterprises, LLC,
Bethesda, Maryland. © 1999 by Discovery Communications, Inc.

Further resources for students and educators available at
www.discoveryschool.com

Designed by Bill SMITH STUDIO
Creative Director: Ron Leighton
Designers: Eric Hoffsten, Jay Jaffe, Brian Kobberger, Nick Stone,
    Sonia Gaube
Production Director: Peter Lindstrom
Photo Editor: Justine Price
Art Buyer: Lillie Caporlingua

Gareth Stevens Editor: Betsy Rasmussen
Gareth Stevens Art Director: Tammy Gruenewald
Technical Advisor: Sara Bruening

Printed in the United States of America

1 2 3 4 5 6 7 8 9 08 07 06 05 04

Writers: Carol Harrison, David Krasnow

Editors: Jackie Ball, Marc Gave

Photographs: Cover, © Tony Stone Images; p. 10, Alexander
Hamilton, © Brown Brothers, Ltd.; p. 11, plane, © USAF
(Reserve)/The National Hurricane Center; p. 12, Dr. Cline,
courtesy of the Rosenberg Library, Galveston, Texas;
p. 12, Galveston, Texas, © M.E. Warren Collection/Photo
Researchers, Inc.; p. 20 Wilson Bentley, courtesy of the
Jericho (Vermont) Historical Society; p. 26, Dr. Susan Solomon,
courtesy of Dr. Susan Solomon/NOAA; p. 27, McMurdo
Station, © Lynn Teo Simarski/NSF.

Illustrations: pp. 4–5, 19, Patricia J. Wynne; pp. 9, 22–23, Joe LeMonnier; p. 20,
    hexagonal snowflake, © R.B. Hoity/Photo Researchers, Inc.;
    p. 21, needle, elaborately branched, fern-like dendrite and
    lop-sided snowflakes, courtesy of the Jericho (Vermont)
    Historical Society.

Acknowledgments: p. 13, telegram exerpted from Storms,
    Floods and Sunshine by J.M. Cline, Pelican Press, Inc.,
    New Orleans, 1945.

Discovery CHANNEL SCHOOL SCIENCE

CONTENTS

You probably don't pay much attention to the weather unless it's doing something you don't like. Maybe you're at a picnic and a thunderstorm blows in, leaving you drenched—and diving for cover. Maybe the airplane you're flying in hits air pockets, making your stomach queasy. Or worst of all, maybe high humidity does a number on your hair. What can you do?

Well, the truth is that you can't do much about changing the weather. But with the wonders of modern technology, you can get a handle on its patterns in your corner of Earth and try to prepare yourself for what's coming. In WEATHER AND CLIMATE, Discovery Channel gives you a close look at the extremes of weather from fair-weather clouds to the destructive forces of hurricanes and tornadoes. You'll never think of weather the same way again!

WEATHER AND CLIMATE

Death Spiral . . . See page 16

Weather &

Have you ever been caught in a thunderstorm? If so, you probably wish you could have had warning in time to head for shelter. But you can develop your own early-warning system. When you look up into the sky, knowing which weather signs to look for can often help you make sensible decisions. Ancient Greeks believed that a thunderstorm occurred when their chief god, Zeus, went into battle. They accounted for the spectacular and deadly phenomenon of lightning by his hurling lightning bolts down from Mount Olympus. But we've learned a lot about the science of weather since then. Here's how wind and water join forces to make a storm.

WINDS IN THE ATMOSPHERE

COOL AIR SINKS

CLOUDS FORM

5

4

3

WIND CYCLE

1 Sunlight hits the earth and the warm, moist air rises.

2 Air nearby rushes in to take the place of the rising warm air, creating wind on the ground.

3 The warm, moist, and rising air cools and forms clouds in the sky.

4 Cool air in the atmosphere sinks toward the ground.

5 Surrounding air rushes in to fill the space left by the sinking cool air, creating winds high in the atmosphere.

FRONT LINE of advancing temperature change, with a warm wind producing a warm front and a cold wind producing a cold front.

WARM AIR RISES

EVAPORATION

1

1

WINDS ON THE GROUND

2

Climate

TROPOSPHERE—Lowest layer of the atmosphere, from sea level to 10 miles (16 km) high, in which most weather events take place.

STRATOSPHERE—Layer of the atmosphere above the troposphere, in which high clouds and very thin air are found.

THUNDERHEAD—Another name for a cumulonimbus cloud, inside which a thunderstorm is formed. It can be 10 miles (16 km) high and contain powerful winds that blow water droplets and bits of ice miles up and down.

THUNDER—The sound caused by a scorching-hot bolt of electricity flashing through the air, which instantly becomes five times hotter than the surface of the Sun. Air molecules spread out at a violent speed, and when they crash back together, you get thunder.

LIGHTNING—Water droplets rub against each other on their way up and down, building positive and negative electrical charges on the clouds. When the difference in the charged areas of the sky becomes too great, a giant electrical spark leaps from one part of the sky to another, or from the sky to the ground (or vice versa). The greater the electrical charge, the more powerful the lightning. And it is hot!

On the ground below the cloud, an electrical charge builds up, which people can sometimes feel in the air. Sometimes it raises the hair on your neck or arms. Strands of hair on your head may stand on end. This is a signal that lightning is about to strike nearby.

3

WATER DROPS FORM

CONDENSATION

2

PRECIPITATION

4

THE WATER CYCLE

1. Evaporation—Water on the earth warms up and enters the air as water vapor.

2. Condensation—As the water vapor rises more, it cools, forming tiny water droplets that, when dense enough, we see as clouds.

3. The water droplets bump against each other and join together, forming water drops.

4. Precipitation—When the water drops become too heavy to float, they fall to the earth.

RAIN—Precipitation in the form of liquid.

SLEET—Rain that freezes.

SNOW—Small ice crystals that form around dust or salt particles.

HAIL—Frozen rain that is circulated up and down in a cloud until it is a hard, frozen ball of ice.

THE RAIN MAN

Q: Hello, and welcome to Weather or Not, the talk show that's taking the country by storm. State your name and age for our audience, please.

A: First name, Drop. Middle name, of. Last name, Water. Sometimes known as Rain. And as for my age, you have a heck of a nerve! That is a totally illegal question. But I'll tell you anyway: I am billions of years old.

Q: Come on!

A: Oh, I know I don't look it . . .

Q: But nothing is that old—especially a drop of water! I mean, rain drops only last until they fall to Earth and then—splat! You're history.

A: That's just the point. I AM history. I've been around forever, and I do mean around. The same water has been going around and around ever since there was first water on Earth.

Q: Really?

A: Yep. No more, no less.

Q: So what's the secret of your long life?

A: One word: change. Keep changing and you'll never feel old. You'll never have time to feel old. Change your name. Change your form. Change your location. Change your underwear.

Q: But what's wrong with the form you're in now? You look OK to me. Round. Bubble-like. Kinda quivery.

A: There's nothing particularly wrong with it, for a drop of water. But my other forms have certain advantages.

Q: Like what?

A: Like stealth. Sneakiness. Being able to disappear into thin air. That's what happens when I turn into a gas.

Q: That does sound like fun, Drop.

A: You mean Vapor—Water Vapor—and actually, it's very uncomfortable. One minute I'm making a nice soft landing on the surface of an ocean or a river, just plopping into the big pool of megatrillions of drops already collected there, and the next . . . the next . . . the Sun comes out! How do you think that makes me feel?

Q: Uh, hot?

A: Hot is not the word. Boiling. Steaming. The heat makes water molecules start moving faster and faster, pushing and shoving, trying to get some space, like too many people jammed into an elevator. It's exhausting, but pretty soon—it works! We spread out so far that there are big spaces between us. Now we're less dense. Lighter than air. We drift from Earth in a big warm happy moist mass up into the troposphere. WHAT a relief!

Q: But where's the troposphere?

A: It's the lowest layer in Earth's atmosphere. Anywhere from sea level to 10 miles (16 kilometers) up. The farther you get up into it, the colder it is. When water vapor gets to where the temperature is around freezing, it starts to condense. Water vapor changes from a gas back into a liquid—tiny droplets of water. LOTS of tiny droplets of water. Millions of droplets in each individual drop. Billions and billions and billions and billions and billions of droplets . . .

Q: I get it, I get it. Quite a crowd!

A: You mean, quite a cloud. Because that's what happens next. All the droplets condense around dust particles floating around up there and form a cloud. Sometimes the cloud is all puffy and fluffy and billowy. That kind of cloud looks white because water droplets reflect light. But sometimes the droplets get really thick and really dense—so thick and dense that we make a cloud that light can't get through.

Q: A dark cloud?

A: Right. A storm cloud. A cloud that gets so thick and heavy that finally it can't stay up there anymore. So it doesn't. It breaks up and falls back down to Earth as precipitation called . . .

Q: I know! Rain!

A: Wrong. Well, not entirely. The precipitation COULD be rain. That's always fine with me, since I like getting back to my liquid form. But if the cloud is high enough and the temperature is just right, the precipitation could be snow. Or ice, my solid form, and the form I like the best. People really pay attention to ice. They give it some respect. Vapor, they can't even see.

And sometimes I think they take water for granted. Even though they couldn't live without it.

Q: Well, Drop, you certainly have had a long, interesting life. Any thoughts for the future?

A: The future, the past, the present, they're all one and the same when you're a drop of water. Round and round the cycle goes, never stops, never slows, know what I mean? But after all these years, I'm used to it. And it's fun never knowing where I'll turn up. I could be in the ocean or a pond or a mud puddle. I could turn up in the plants in your garden. Or in an animal. In fact, you're mostly water yourself, so you could be my very next home. But I'll just be passing through. You'll lose me through evaporation, when you sweat. Or you'll lose me when you . . .

Q: Er, let's not get personal. See you around . . . and around . . . and around. . . . and around . . .

Activity

GLASS ACT Fill a glass with ice water. In a few minutes, jot down what you notice happening both on the inside and the outside of the glass. What do you think is the connection between the two? Now fill another glass with ice water. Add a few drops of food coloring. In a few minutes, what color is the water on the outside of the glass? Where did this water come from? Read what you wrote earlier. Have your thoughts about what was happening changed?

WILD and WOOLLY WEATHER

I CAN'T TAKE THIS PRESSURE

Low Pressure When air warms up, the air molecules spread out so there are fewer air molecules in the same space. Warm air weighs less than cool air, which means that warm air presses down on Earth less than cool air. Less pressing equals low pressure. A mass of warming air is an area of low pressure. Warm air rises and produces clouds, so low pressure areas usually bring rain or storms.

High Pressure When air cools, the air molecules bunch together so there are more air molecules in the same space. The air mass becomes heavier and sinks toward Earth, creating an area of high pressure. More pressing equals high pressure. No clouds are formed in this process, so clear skies and fair weather usually come with a high pressure area.

Measurement of air pressure is done with a barometer. This instrument measures the weight of air on one square inch of surface area at sea level. The measure is given in inches, because the early barometers were set up to see how many inches high the pressure would push a column of mercury.

BLOWING HOT AND COLD

The three temperature scales we use are Fahrenheit, Celsius (also known as Centigrade), and Kelvin, named after their inventors. In the United States, Fahrenheit is commonly used to record air and body temperatures. Celsius is used in most of the world, where the metric system is used. Kelvin is for scientific use. Here's how they stack up:

System	Fahrenheit	Celsius	Kelvin
Boiling point of water (at sea level)	212°	100°	373°
Normal human body temperature	98.6°	37°	310°
Comfortable room temperature	70°	21°	294°
Freezing point of water (at sea level)	32°	0°	273°
Absolute zero (the coldest anything can theoretically be)	-460°	-273°	0°

Measuring Up

Barometers measure air pressure.

Thermometers measure air temperature.

Anemometers measure wind speed.

Psychrometers and **Hygrometers** measure humidity, the amount of water vapor in the air.

Rain gauges measure precipitation.

Sunshine recorders measure hours of sunshine in a day.

Weather balloons take temperature, humidity, and pressure readings in the atmosphere and transmit data to weather stations on the ground.

Famous U.S. Weather Disasters

Year	Type	Location	Damage	Lives Lost
1888	Blizzard ("Blizzard of '88")	Maryland to Maine	200 ships sunk, buildings and trains buried under 40- to 50-foot snowdrifts	400+
1925	Tri-State Tornado	Missouri, Illinois, Indiana	$18 million (1925 dollars)	695
1988	Drought/Heat Wave	Central and Eastern U.S.	$40 billion	5,000+
1992	Hurricane Andrew	Florida, Louisiana	$27 billion	58
1993	Great Midwest Flood	Central U.S.	$21 billion	48

How Close Is That Thunderstorm?

Thunder happens at about the same time as lightning, but from a distance you see the lightning first because light travels much faster than sound. To find how far away the storm is, try this "flash to bang" technique:

Count the number of seconds from a "flash" of lightning to the "bang" of thunder. Divide that number by five, because sound travels one mile in five seconds. If you counted eight seconds from flash to bang, the storm would be about 1.6 miles (2.6 km) away.

To find out if a storm is coming closer or moving away, use the "flash to bang" technique again in a minute or two. If the second time is shorter, the storm is getting closer. If the second time is longer, the storm is moving away. A thunderstorm usually can't be heard more than 10 miles (16 km) away, although you may see the lightning.

whirl winds

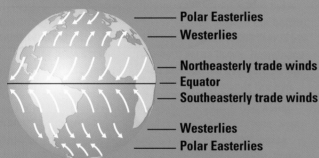

——— Polar Easterlies
——— Westerlies

——— Northeasterly trade winds
——— Equator
——— Southeasterly trade winds

——— Westerlies
——— Polar Easterlies

Weather changes with the wind. The air doesn't stand still for long because air temperature varies with the uneven heating of the earth by the Sun and produces the world's wind patterns.

1. The equator receives the Sun's rays most directly. The warmed air expands and rises.
2. Cooler air flows in from the poles to take the place of the rising air. Winds are created that flow toward the equator, but not in a straight path. Because Earth is spinning, the winds end up curving toward the east in the Northern Hemisphere and toward the west in the Southern Hemisphere. This is called the Coriolis effect.

The jet streams are paths of high-speed wind moving at 100 to 200 miles per hour (161 to 322 kph) that flow around Earth at approximately 30,000 feet (9,144 m)—about as high as the highest clouds.

Bends and loops in the jet stream change often, and the position of the jet stream affects the weather in the atmosphere below. Low pressure areas, where storms form, often occur under a bend in the jet stream.

Lightning Safety Tips

Lightning can strike even when it's not raining. Thunderstorms can also produce hail, high winds, heavy rain, flooding, and tornadoes.

AT HOME

▶ Stay away from doors and windows, metal sinks and faucets, radiators, and the phone unless you're making an emergency call.

▶ Take off headsets and turn off computers, TVs, and appliances.

IN OPEN COUNTRY

▶ Crouch (rather than lie) in a ditch or other low area with your hands around your knees or head, so your body has the least possible contact with the ground.

▶ Keep at least 15 feet (4.5 m) from other people. If lightning strikes nearby, it can travel along the ground from person to person.

▶ Stay away from water, metal fences or poles, and tall objects including trees, picnic shelters, or buildings that stand alone.

▶ Don't hold a golf club, a fishing pole, or an umbrella.

▶ Don't resume outdoor activities until half an hour after the thunder and lightning have stopped.

LIGHTNING FAST FACTS

▶ Ninety percent of lightning flashes happen within a cloud or between clouds.

▶ Lightning strikes the earth somewhere in the world about one hundred times every minute.

▶ An average of nine thousand fires a year are started by lightning in U.S. forests and grasslands.

▶ Your chances of being hit by lightning are very low. Some estimates put the odds at 1 in 350,000. Other estimates put the odds at 1 in 600,000.

▶ Nevertheless, 325 to 500 people in the United States are struck by lightning each year.

▶ Lightning comes in a variety of forms. What do you think each of these looks like? Anvil, ball, bead, heat, ribbon, sheet, staccato, streak (or forked).

DESOLATION ROW

Galveston, Texas, September, 1900

Early in the twentieth century, before instant satellite weather updates, forecasters had to rely mostly on the telegraph to exchange information. On September 4, the Central Office of the U.S. Weather Bureau in Washington, D.C., received messages from ships at sea and weather observers on islands that a tropical storm was moving north through the Caribbean Sea. On the afternoon of September 6, the barometer began to fall slowly but steadily.

THOUSANDS SAVED IN GALVESTON BY DR. CLINE

The hurricane that swept Galveston on the evening of September 8, 1900, left 8,000 dead and 5,000 injured. Two-thirds of the city's buildings were washed away, including more than 3,600 homes. It is the worst hurricane disaster recorded in the United States.

The number of casualties in Galveston and neighboring towns would have been even greater had it not been for the warnings given out by Dr. Isaac Cline, Head Observer of the Galveston Weather Bureau. In addition to sending messages over the telephone and telegraph on the morning of the eighth, Dr. Cline drove his horse and cart through the flooded streets of the beachfront community, warning hundreds of citizens to escape to higher ground.

The condition of thousands of those who have been spared is far more pitiable than that of the dead. Their resources have been swept away by wind and tide, and they are desolate in the midst of desolation.

—Joel Chandler Harris, noted author

Dr. Isaac Cline

TELEGRAM

September 23, 1900

On the morning of the seventh, the Central Office in Washington issued storm warnings for Galveston, and signal flags were raised on the roof of the Weather Bureau building downtown to alert the people of the city. Cirrus clouds moved across the blue sky from the southeast, and during the afternoon a heavy swell from the southeast made its appearance in the Gulf of Mexico.

Both were signs of an approaching tropical storm, but the forecaster at the Central Office thought the hurricane would make landfall before it got to Galveston.

By early morning on the eighth, the tide had risen to an unusual height considering that the wind was from the north and northwest. Several inches of water stood in the yards and streets five blocks from the beach. Rain showers commenced at 8:45 A.M., and the storm tide continued to rise.

Cline telegraphed his weather observations to Washington, but the forecaster in the Central Office never issued an official hurricane warning or emergency warnings for Galveston. Against Weather Bureau policy, Cline and his staff spread the word that great danger was approaching.

Dense clouds and heavy rains were in evidence by noon. The wagon bridge and the railroad bridge connecting the island with the mainland were going under water. The barometer fell to 29.42 inches and continued falling rapidly.

By 3:30 P.M., telephone and telegraph wires had gone down. The entire island was covered with two to four feet of water.

Storm winds from the northeast increased steadily to hurricane velocity by late afternoon. Pieces of slate roofing and heavy boards torn from buildings blew through the streets, killing many in the beachfront area who only now were trying to escape to higher ground in the center of town.

The anemometer on the roof of the Weather Bureau building blew away at 6:15 P.M. after registering winds of 100 mph (160 kph). Water was 4 to 5 feet (1 to 1.5 m) deep on the streets of the beach community.

By 7:30 P.M. houses several blocks from the beach stood in 10 feet (3 m) of water. Buildings on the beachfront were swept from their foundations and smashed together, creating piles of debris 15 feet (4.5 m) high that the waves used like battering rams to crush buildings farther inland. After 8:00 P.M., the wind came with an even greater fury for the next three hours, attaining an estimated velocity of at least 120 miles (193 km) per hour. The barometer fell to 28.53 inches.

Around 11:00 P.M. the wind steadily diminished and the water began to fall. At dawn on the morning of the ninth, the tide was nearly normal under a clear sky with light winds from the south. But sunrise revealed one of the most horrible sights that ever a civilized people have looked upon.

I. M. Cline

Activity

THEN AND NOW Refer to the hurricane chart on page 11 and determine the category of the Galveston Hurricane, which took place before the category system was developed. Look at the disaster chart on page 8 and compare the number of lives lost in the Galveston Hurricane with those lost in the Category 4 hurricane that hit Louisiana in 1992. What does this difference indicate? What do we have today (that Isaac Cline didn't have) to help us forecast and prepare for a hurricane? How could we improve our safety measures?

LET'S GO FOR A SPIN

A powerful tornado—a whirling column of wind—can leave an 18-wheeler twisted by the side of the road like a drinking straw. When you hear a tornado warning, or when you see the sky turn a funny color (greenish, for example), you want to get to safety. Not Daphne Zaras. That's when she hits the road.

Daphne Zaras

If you've seen the movie *Twister*, here's a surprise: Even though it was fiction, some scientists really do chase tornadoes. One is Daphne Zaras, a meteorologist with the National Severe Storms Laboratory in Norman, Oklahoma. Zaras participates in VORTEX, the Verification of the Origins of Rotation in Tornadoes EXperiment. In other words, why do the things start spinning around like crazy? And why does Zaras want to be there when they do?

"Most of the ideas on how tornadoes form involve the air up close to where they happen," she says. "The only way to prove or disprove each of the hypotheses is to go there and try to measure what's going on." Since there's no way to stop a tornado, understanding tornadoes to predict them better is the key to preventing deaths.

Easier said than done! Twisters are tricky. Teams of intrepid scientists have to drive fast to catch them in action. They get close enough, about one-half mile (.8 km), to get lashed by dust clouds and winds that can overturn a car. One chase vehicle had its windshield smashed by softball-sized hail. What if the tornado takes a wrong turn—toward them? Says Zaras, "We have at least two people helping to navigate. We have to have road options to get out of dangerous situations fast! So we are always thinking ahead about our strategy just in case a tornado, strong winds, or large hail change direction." Apparently the method works, because despite some close calls, no one on VORTEX has been injured.

The teams chase tornadoes with cars called mobile mesonet vehicles. Each has a ski rack mounted on top that carries sensors to measure wind speed and direction, temperature, dew point, pressure, and latitude–longitude position. All the data is logged into a laptop computer inside the car. The mesonet vehicles try to surround the area under the storm where a tornado seems to be forming.

"Think about this problem," Zaras reflects. "You have a moving, evolving storm, but cars needing good locations of roads. What if the storm moves over a large farm right when it starts to produce the tornado? You might not be able to keep the cars around the tornado because the roads don't go through the barn!"

The first leg of VORTEX, in 1994 and 1995, produced a new hypothesis about tornadogenesis, the creation of tornadoes. In 1999, the team hit the road again to test it out. Zaras reports: "Spring is a *very* busy time for us. Not only are we continuing our studies of past events, but we are chasing new storms. We also spend time talking to TV show and news producers. Everyone is interested in seeing what the latest ideas are in the science during the spring, when severe weather is on their mind. We also do a lot of public education on how to be safe during severe weather."

In the field, the team also reports to the National Weather Service, helping to spread the warning to people in the tornado's path.

"We have to wait for storm systems to cross the Rocky Mountains. Once they do, we are sometimes able to chase several days in a row. We like to chase close enough to home that we can drive home that night and sleep in our own beds, but sometimes we extend our chases as far as Nebraska. It's easy to put six hundred or more miles on the car in one day while you are storm chasing."

Chasing tornadoes isn't always an action-adventure movie, though. Patience is high on the list of requirements. "There's a lot of 'hurry up and wait,'" Zaras points out. "The target area—where we think tornadoes will form—is usually two or more hours drive away. That part of the chase can be relaxing, but once we get to the target area we sometimes have to wait for the storms to form. We often toss footballs or Frisbees around. We compare readings between cars to make sure all the instruments are calibrated to one another. Once storms form, we start working on intercept strategy by studying the maps and looking carefully at the storm. How long before it might become tornadic? Is there a good road network where the storm seems to be headed? If the answer is 'no,' then we often look for another storm nearby which can be followed for a while."

When a storm is about to produce a tornado, the cloud base changes very rapidly. "There is always some kind of fast spinning and often very rapidly rising cloud. Then we start to watch the ground underneath that spot for dirt and debris: most tornadoes become tornadoes before the funnel cloud shows up. The average lifetime of a tornado is only seven minutes, so we have to be in place right away to get good data, and we stay all around it through its lifetime. After it dissipates, we watch carefully to see if the storm will produce another one. These special storms called supercell thunderstorms often live for several hours and produce more than one tornado."

If the storm forms outside the target area, the chase teams literally may race against the wind. "Sometimes they don't form at all, and we end up driving home in clear blue skies."

It can be boring, but it's often dangerous. Zaras knows that if a twister gets hold of her mobile mesonet vehicle, the car—and she—might land in a heap hundreds of feet away. Why bother? "The weather is complicated and always challenging," she says. "It's so exciting to see science in action."

What's in YOUR Forecast?

In places where severe weather occurs frequently, the National Weather Service relies on a network of volunteers called spotters. Tornado spotters are amateurs who are trained to recognize tornado conditions and warning signs. When the National Weather Service puts them on alert, they keep watch and report any activity by telephone, cell phone, or ham radio. Their work is especially valuable in the "tornado alley" of Texas, Oklahoma, Kansas, and the Mississippi River Valley, where warm, moist air from the Gulf of Mexico and high-pressure air moving southeast from Canada lock heads with explosive effects.

Not the adventurous type? There are plenty of safer weather-related jobs. Your local TV or radio meteorologist or weather announcer is probably the most obvious example of this. A meteorologist uses science to observe, understand, explain, and forecast the weather. The military and some government agencies also employ meteorologists.

Atmospheric or climate scientists have similar jobs. Corporations and government agencies usually hire them to monitor pollution from traffic and manufacturing, to study the greenhouse effect, analyze past climates, and predict trends. Most importantly, they often give policy advice on the effects of air pollution and climate on companies and the economy.

Tale of a Twister

"I saw the cloud coming and tried to take shelter inside. But as soon as I reached for the door knob, the house took off into the sky. I wasn't hurt at all."

"I was in a restaurant when the storm hit. First the roof blew away, then all four walls. I was left sitting on the floor."

"Dad wanted to see the storm damage, so we drove over there. What we saw was unbelievable destruction. Houses and barns ripped apart, railroad cars turned over, stands of trees torn to shreds, and bloody clothes and towels hanging outside houses that still stood."

"The injured had been crushed by falling timbers, thrown several yards by the wind, and pierced with sharp splinters of wood."

"After the storm, we had to clean the debris from the wheat fields. We picked up splintered boards and tree branches as well as dead chickens with their feathers blown off and rabbits that looked like they'd been skinned."

—*survivors of the Great Tri-State Tornado*

On the afternoon of March 18, 1925, thousands of people in Missouri, Indiana, and Illinois experienced one of the most devastating weather disasters on record. A huge, powerful tornado ripped across a section of the three states, completely destroying four towns, killing 695 people and injuring 2,000 more.

With a path of destruction sometimes more than a mile wide, the Tri-State Tornado was one of the largest in history. For most of its life, this tornado looked like a large thundercloud rather than a twisting funnel. People had very little, if any, advance warning, and some never knew what hit them. The tornado ripped down phone lines as it passed, so there was no way for survivors to alert others.

There was no radar to detect the tornado, no computers to plot its probable path, and no TV or radio weather reports to warn people of the approaching storm.

Even today, meteorologists are unable to measure a tornado's wind speed because of the intense violence of the winds in the funnel. After a tornado has passed, its strength and size are determined by observing the type of damage it caused. The Fujita Tornado Intensity Scale ranks tornadoes and estimates their wind speeds according to their destructiveness. The Tri-State has been ranked an F5 tornado.

Tornado Safety

AT HOME
- Stay in a basement or small windowless area on the first floor, such as a hall, a closet, or under the stairs.
- Stay away from windows and doors.
- Use heavy furniture for shelter or cover yourself with a blanket.
- Leave a mobile home and seek shelter in a sturdy building.

OUTSIDE
- Leave your car and find a ditch or shallow area to lie in.
- Cover your head with your hands for protection from flying objects.

THE GREAT TORNADO
of March 18, 1925

541 killed and 1,423 seriously injured in 40 minutes

Missouri

Illinois

Indiana

Kentucky

72 mph
67 mph
60 mph
56 mph
60 mph
73 mph

MT. VERNON

GRIFFIN 100% Destroyed
PARRISH 90% Destroyed
WEST FRANKFURT 20% Destroyed
DeSOTO 30% Destroyed
MURPHYSBORO 40% Destroyed
GORHAM 100% Destroyed
ANNAPOLIS 90% Destroyed
ELLINGTON
CAIRO

0 10 20 30 40 50

N

Fujita Tornado Intensity Scale

Ranking	Wind Speed	Type of Damage
F0	**40–72 mph** (64–116 kph)	**LIGHT:** branches broken off trees, shallow-rooted trees pushed over, signs damaged, some windows broken
F1	**73–112 mph** (117–180 kph)	**MODERATE:** roof surfaces peeled off, mobile homes overturned, moving cars pushed off roads, garages or sheds destroyed, trees snapped or broken
F2	**113–157 mph** (182–253 kph)	**SIGNIFICANT:** Roofs torn off, mobile homes demolished, boxcars overturned, large trees broken or uprooted, light objects blown through the air
F3	**158–206 mph** (254–331 kph)	**SEVERE:** Roofs and walls torn off, trains overturned, most trees uprooted, heavy cars lifted off the ground and tossed, weak pavement blown off the road
F4	**207–260 mph** (333–418 kph)	**DEVASTATING:** Homes leveled, forests uprooted, cars thrown and disintegrated, other heavy objects thrown
F5	**261–318 mph** (420–512 kph)	**INCREDIBLE:** Sturdy homes carried large distances and disintegrated, steel-reinforced concrete buildings badly damaged, cars and other heavy objects blown the distance of a football field, trees debarked

Activity

RECORDS At this writing, the Tri-State Tornado still holds the records for the longest tornado track, the longest continuous time on the ground, and the number of deaths caused. Study the map and determine how many miles the Tri-State tornado traveled. What was its average speed? Use that information to figure out the record length of time this tornado existed.

HEAD IN THE CLOUDS

You don't have to chase after a tornado to learn something about the weather. But you can see, and feel, a lot when you're high up in the sky. If you've ever flown in an airplane, you have most likely seen clouds up close. But how about getting closer? How about spending a few seconds being caught in a cloud that's spawning a whirlwind of 300 mph (nearly 483 kmph)? Hang on tight!

As you take off in our balloon, the sky is a bright, deep blue, and there's a light breeze. The Sun is so warm that you don't notice any change in temperature, even though the air is getting cooler. About 3,000 feet (914 m) above the ground, you have your first close encounter of the cloud kind. **Cumulus clouds ❶**, those billowy, fair-weather friends, are floating through the sky like huge, puffy boats.

They look like dry, fluffy cotton candy—but they're wet inside. Of course you knew that clouds are made of drops of water, and ice crystals if it's cold enough. But don't despair. You can dry off. And your balloon knows just where and how to go.

Up, up you soar on a light breeze, out into the clear sky—until you hit a whole bunch of clouds. A cloud bank! Will you ever get out of those **stratocumulus clouds ❷**?

Sure. Another upward wind, more sky, then more cumulus-style clouds. These **altocumulus ("high" cumulus) clouds ❸** are more than one mile (1.6 km) above Earth. You can't tell from here, but they are "leaking." Watch out! Showers below.

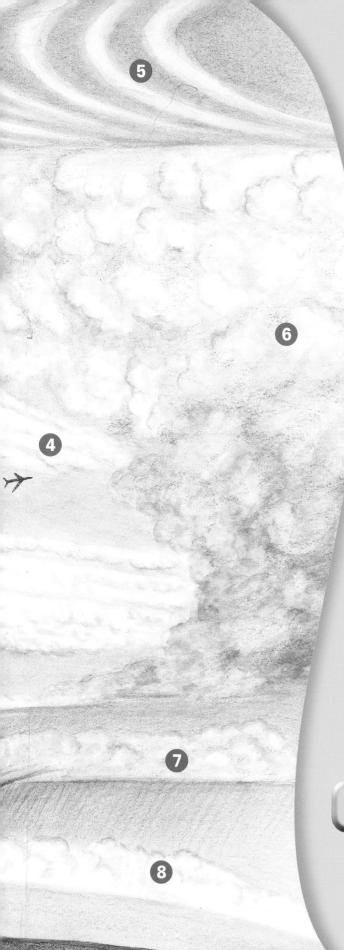

You're relaxing more now and really starting to enjoy the ride. As you soar to 20,000 feet (6,094 m), you see some open sky. You're among clouds again, but they're thin, white, and wavy. Holy Mackerel! They're **cirrostratus clouds 4**, also called a mackerel sky. What's that you see? Showers? Never mind. You're still climbing high into the sky.

Now you're really soaring. At 30,000 feet (9,144 m), the clouds are thinning and you can see the brilliant blue sky above. These **cirrus clouds 5** are nothing more than wisps, with curled and curved ends. If only you could see anything below you besides all those other clouds!

Well, you've gone as high as your balloon will take you, and now you're descending ever so slightly— until—whoosh! You're caught up in what seems to be a cloud storm. That's not surprising, because you're inside a storm cloud or, rather, clouds. These **cumulonimbus clouds 6** really mean business! Flash! Boom! No wonder another name for this kind of cloud is thunderhead. And don't be surprised if your cloud is also sending down hail. It's a real meanie. It can even produce tornadoes when it wants to!

You don't like this cloud much, and there seems to be no end to it—and all its friends. But suddenly— whoa! Hold on to your hat! You're really moving. Out, out, out of that storm cloud. And down, down, down. Your stomach is feeling more than a tad queasy.

What lies between you and the ground, where you're headed now at a rapid clip, so that you're only about 4,000 feet (1,219 m) above it? Suddenly it's darker, and you know it isn't nighttime. You're in a **nimbostratus cloud 7**, that's what. Nimbo or nimbus in a cloud name means "rain." And that's exactly what's falling through the sky, along with your balloon.

You're almost down to the ground. But there's more gray stuff and light rain. **Stratus 8** is the lowest of the low. Sometimes it reaches right down to the ground. That's what fog really is—stratus clouds scraping the tops of skyscrapers, and even your nose.

Happy landings!

Activity

LOOK UP Every day for a week, go outside at the same time. Observe the clouds. Record what kind of clouds you see and the type of weather in general. At the end of the week, go back over your record and try to see the weather patterns that different clouds indicated.

The White Stuff

I t's white, it falls from the sky, and pretty quickly it turns to mucky slush. Bet that's all you know about snow.

Snow is not frozen rain. That's sleet, and it's a lot less pretty. In fact, a lot of our rain was snow that melted as it fell. Snow is a crystal of ice that forms around a microscopic particle of dust or bacteria in the atmosphere. Temperatures are generally less than 5° F (-15° C) when snow forms (it's much colder up there!).

To freeze, at least three boomerang-shaped water molecules link up in a way that creates a six-sided shape. Then the crystal begins to "grow" as molecule after molecule of water vapor attach themselves. As the snowflake drifts around, wind, humidity, and especially temperature cause it to grow in different shapes. Mathematicians have studied snowflakes as examples of fractals, complex structures built of basic identical units. (By the way, there's no scientific proof that every snowflake is unique. But try finding two identical snowflakes. We bet you'll be inside looking for hot chocolate long before it happens.)

Say Cheese

Wilson A. Bentley could be called the father of snow—or at least of snow photography. Bentley was a Vermont farmer and self-taught photographer who

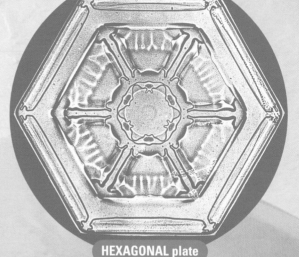

HEXAGONAL plate

invented ways to photograph an individual snowflake through a microscope. He kept at his project for forty-seven years, producing thousands of pictures. His book *Snow Crystals*, written with W. J. Humphreys in 1931, amazed people with the intricate beauty of nature and turned snowflake photography into a popular hobby.

In 1951, the Commission of Snow and Ice of the International Association of Hydrology (the study of water) adopted a classification system for snow crystals. They identified seven basic types: plates, star shapes, columns, needles, spatial dendrites (branched crystals), capped columns, and irregular crystals.

But which type forms where? In the cold, dry air of high cirrus clouds, there is relatively little moisture in the clouds. With fewer molecules to attach to each flake, snowflakes under these conditions are usually simple plates or six-sided columns. A plate may attach to one or both ends of a column.

Low clouds, where plenty of moisture allows flakes to grow large, form a variety of

Wilson A. Bentley

crystal shapes, depending mostly on temperature. This is where the more beautiful dendrites form.

Flakes have sharper tips when temperatures are colder; they grow more quickly and stay frozen. Crisp branched forms that look like ferns grow in colder clouds. In warmer temperatures they may melt and refreeze, forming smoother, more rounded shapes.

Warmer temperatures may produce needle shapes, which are columns that don't grow right.

If crystals are growing in clouds with heavy winds, they encounter different atmospheric conditions as they grow. This causes them to become irregular.

NEEDLE snowflake

ELABORATELY branched dendrite snowflake

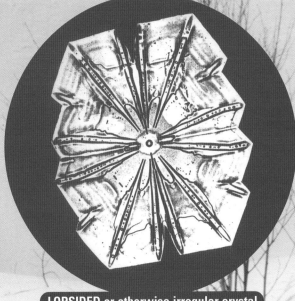

LOPSIDED or otherwise irregular crystal

FERNLIKE dendrite

Activity

THE POWER OF OBSERVATION Looking at snow isn't easy. Your microscope must be chilled way below zero or it will melt the flake. However, you can capture a drop of rain or a particle of soil to see what secrets it will yield. Examine something very tiny from your environment under a microscope and make a sketch to record what you see.

It Takes All Kinds

If an alien scientist studying Earth came up to you and asked what the weather was like yesterday, chances are you might say, "It was sunny and warm, with a light breeze" or some other kind of short description. But if that alien asked you what the weather was like all last year, you would have to stop and think hard. How would you describe something over such a long period —something that may go through a number of changes?

What you'd need to do is to describe the climate, the average weather pattern, over the course of a year. The climate of an area is determined by a combination of factors, including the amount of sunlight it receives, the height of the land, nearby ocean currents, and world wind patterns. There are several main climate areas. These in turn can be broken down into smaller, more specific climate areas.

TOP 10—WELL, 11— EXTREME WEATHER SPOTS

RAIN ❶ Lloro, Colombia, and ❷ Mawsynram, India, sometimes get more than 460 inches (1,168 centimeters) of rain in a year.

THUNDERSTORMS ❸ Java, Indonesia, and ❹ Tororo, Uganda, average more than 250 days per year with thunderstorms.

FOG ❺ Grand Banks, Newfoundland, Canada, averages 120 days of fog per year.

WIND ❻ At Mount Washington, New Hampshire, winds have been clocked at 231 miles per hour (372 kph).

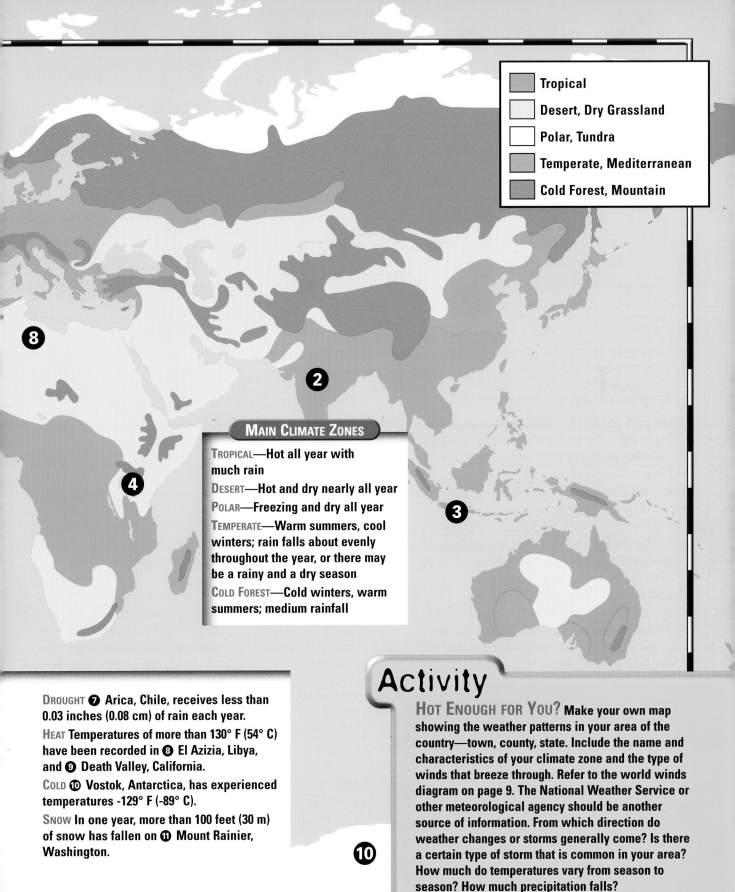

Legend:
- Tropical
- Desert, Dry Grassland
- Polar, Tundra
- Temperate, Mediterranean
- Cold Forest, Mountain

MAIN CLIMATE ZONES

TROPICAL—Hot all year with much rain

DESERT—Hot and dry nearly all year

POLAR—Freezing and dry all year

TEMPERATE—Warm summers, cool winters; rain falls about evenly throughout the year, or there may be a rainy and a dry season

COLD FOREST—Cold winters, warm summers; medium rainfall

DROUGHT **7** Arica, Chile, receives less than 0.03 inches (0.08 cm) of rain each year.

HEAT Temperatures of more than 130° F (54° C) have been recorded in **8** El Azizia, Libya, and **9** Death Valley, California.

COLD **10** Vostok, Antarctica, has experienced temperatures -129° F (-89° C).

SNOW In one year, more than 100 feet (30 m) of snow has fallen on **11** Mount Rainier, Washington.

Activity

HOT ENOUGH FOR YOU? Make your own map showing the weather patterns in your area of the country—town, county, state. Include the name and characteristics of your climate zone and the type of winds that breeze through. Refer to the world winds diagram on page 9. The National Weather Service or other meteorological agency should be another source of information. From which direction do weather changes or storms generally come? Is there a certain type of storm that is common in your area? How much do temperatures vary from season to season? How much precipitation falls?

WHERE IN

Weather events like El Niño and La Niña can cause drought, long spells with no rain. Places where low rainfall is the normal climate—under 10 inches (25 cm), by most definitions—are deserts. They are not all lifeless wastes of sand. Many of the deserts in Arizona, for example, are beautiful and full of unique plant and animal life. What these places have in common is that something prevents them from receiving much rain. Generally, either mountains get in the way of moist air, or high pressure prevents clouds from forming. You find yourself in a desert now. But which one?

Your throat is parched, the hair on your arms is standing up, and you shiver in the brisk wind. You've been walking for days, and your damp shirt clings to your back, chilling your skin. The ground is cracked. Hardly anything seems to be alive in the rocky ground. Your water and food supplies are dwindling.

You started in a valley east of here. Looking through your telescope toward the east you saw a high mountain range whose slopes were green, a few capped with snow. But they look much too high for you to cross, so you turned in the other direction. Hiking over rough, rocky land, you've steered a course due west following your compass and the Sun's path. With half a day's detour, you found a pass in another, lower range of mountains. Even there, you found hardly a stream, and what you found was salty. You're happy to come across a rocky pool with a bit of moss around the sides; it must have rained sometime in the past few months. On the other side of these hills, you think, you will certainly find water. Thin, high cirrostratus clouds have been dampening the sky for days.

Finally, you come over the last peak, and before you, miles off, lies the ocean. The Sun is just beginning to set on the horizon. To your surprise, the land here is just as dry and barren. But as you begin to get worried, you reach the water's edge. With relief, you put down your backpack and roll up your pants to go splashing and relax your feet. YEEEOOW—that water is freezing! You wouldn't swim in that on the hottest day of the year. Without much Sun to warm you, you might regret getting any wetter, so you just wipe the dust off your neck with a numb hand and strike out to find a town.

A mile or two north, you come across a little fishing boat with a line and hooks. It seems to be abandoned, but it looks safe, so you paddle out to look for dinner. You don't have far to go. The ocean is teeming with fish a hundred yards out, and by attaching a tiny crab you found in the sand to a little hook, you bring in a small bass after your fourth try. The ocean at least will give you water to cook and wash, so you can save your last canteen for tomorrow. A bit of driftwood on the rocks will do for firewood. One of the pieces you find is part of a sign in Spanish. You're set for the night. Gazing up at the stars, you can make out the Southern Cross.

But where are you? Why is it so dry here, so close to the ocean? Locate yourself and explain where you've ended up.

THE WORLD?

Use these clues . . .

Clues

The table below gives some information on the world's deserts. Using this table, the map on pages 22–23, and your knowledge of weather and climate, figure out where you are.

Desert	Average Annual Precipitation	Location
Sahara	less than 5 inches (12.7 cm)	Northern Africa
Gobi	3 inches (7.6 cm) in the west	Mongolia and Northern China, north of Himalayas
Atacama	1 inch (2.5 cm) or less	western coast of Chile
Mojave	less than 5 inches (12.7 cm)	California, east of Sierra Nevada range
Kalahari	6 inches (15.3 cm) in the southwest	Botswana, Namibia, South Africa
Australian	10 inches (25.4 cm) or less	interior highlands and basin of Australia

(Answer on page 32.)

Where the Penguins Roam

The O Zone

Along with temperature, humidity, precipitation, and air pressure, air quality is a fact of life that we have become aware of as pollutants threaten our very atmosphere. You may have heard of ozone, a form of oxygen gas.

"Isn't ozone bad for you?" you may be asking. The answer is, yes and no. In the lower atmosphere, high concentrations of smelly smog ozone gas can cause respiratory problems and disease. Small concentrations found naturally (lightning strikes produce ozone, for example) aren't a problem, but power plants and many industrial processes release gases that can build up ozone. With the wrong weather conditions preventing the gas from dissipating, ozone becomes a major health hazard.

Ozone is most harmful in the stratosphere, where we don't breathe it. There it is our best protector against ultraviolet rays from the Sun. Forget your SPF 30 sunscreen—the ozone layer absorbs radiation and takes it out of the picture. If the ozone layer were to disappear entirely, Earth would be flooded with UV rays cancerous to humans and destructive to much life on the planet.

Ross Island, Antarctica, 1986

What to do about a form of pollution produced mostly in urban areas that may be harmful to people, animals, and plant life? Do some fieldwork to study it—in a place inhabited solely by penguins.

That's what Dr. Susan Solomon did when she led a team of sixteen scientists to Antarctica in 1986. The year before, the British Antarctic Survey had made the alarming discovery of a "hole" over the southernmost continent in the layer of ozone gas that surrounds the stratosphere. Scientists had suspected that the ozone layer might be thinning in the late 1970s, but suddenly the evidence had become frighteningly clear—and worse than anyone thought. The question was, why? And why, of all places, in Antarctica?

Solomon, a chemist with the National Oceanic and Atmospheric Administration (NOAA), jumped at the chance to go. "I was at the right place at the right time," she remarks. Prior to her trip, Solomon had published a paper that showed how clouds of tiny crystals high above the polar region could help pollution damage ozone. Her study was based on a computer model. Suddenly, she says, "I had the opportunity to go to Antarctica to probe the chemistry of the ozone hole with the hard facts of measurements."

Solomon's team from the National Oceanic and Atmospheric Administration went to McMurdo Station (see sidebar at right). They donned parkas and set out to collect

Dr. Susan Solomon, dressed for business.

atmospheric samples and study the weather conditions. She and her group set up a light collecting instrument—somewhat like the light meter used by photographers—on the roof of their hut. They used a mirror to shine rays of the Sun and Moon into the instrument. "One night I did the measurements on my own. About three A.M. it turned cloudy, so I left the tracking mirror on the roof and crawled into my sleeping bag. When I woke up there was a raging blizzard, and I had to rescue the mirror! You couldn't see your hand in front of your face. The wind was so strong it rocked me back and forth, and there I was on the roof. I had never seen anything remotely like it, and I'm from Chicago."

The team's measurements helped prove Solomon's theory. By interpreting the wavelengths of light received by their instrument, they learned that a compound called chlorine dioxide was present in unusually large amounts above Antarctica. The compound, one of a group that comes from chlorofluorocarbons (KLOR oh FLOR oh KAR bins), or CFCs, traces back to aerosol spray cans in bathrooms all over the world. Drifting through the atmosphere, the chlorine gases met ice clouds in the polar region and began breaking up ozone. Solomon's work on the Antarctic Expedition broke new scientific ground in our understanding of how human-produced chemicals can alter the planet's environment profoundly. As a result, she testified before the United States Congress about the need to control chlorine gases. The Montreal Protocol, an international agreement to cooperate on the ozone problem, took place in part because of Solomon's Antarctic Expedition.

"Since that time, my work has taken me south to Antarctica [again in 1987] and north to Greenland. I've always enjoyed challenges and am not afraid to try new things—including slightly crazy things like spending months in the Antarctic. It's beautiful there, so pristine. The stratospheric clouds and the low angle of the Sun make a sunset like nowhere else in the world—purple, salmon, orange, yellow. Antarctica has a special place in my heart."

McMurdo Station, Antarctica's "big city" on Ross Island, has a winter population of about one hundred people. There, the National Science Foundation has a headquarters known as the "chalet" and dozens of smaller buildings to house and supply expeditions like Solomon's with food, computer facilities, and transportation. Arrivals sometimes shuttle from the airfield to McMurdo on trucks with tank treads to grip the snow.

McMurdo Station is on the coast, where ocean waters keep temperatures relatively warm. The annual mean temperature there is 5° to 14° F (-15° to -10° C), which is like Hawaii by South Pole standards. The vast, unmelting sheet of ice and 100-foot- (30-m-) thick snow banks that cover most of the continent reflect about three-fourths of the Sun's rays and keep it from warming up. Temperatures above freezing are almost never recorded; the warmest temperatures at Vostok average -27° F (-33° C), and the lowest temperature here, -129° F (-89.4° C), is the lowest ever recorded on Earth. Penguins and seals along the shores and bacteria in the soil account for most of the natural life on Antarctica.

Activity

KEEPING TRACK Measurement was the key to Solomon's expedition. Take measurements of your own. Use an outdoor thermometer over a one-week period to track the temperature (do at same time or times each day). Explain any changes (or lack of changes) according to what you have learned about weather and climate.

Weathering

TIMELINE

340 B.C.	A.D. 1400s–1700s	1844	Circa 1915	1920s

340 B.C.

Ancient Greek scientist and philosopher Aristotle writes *Meteorologica*, which set out his observations about rain, snow, and other weather events. The word meteorology, which means "the science of weather forecasting," comes from the Greek word *meteoros*, which means "high in the sky."

A.D. 1400s–1700s

Early weather instruments. People start to gather data and make weather forecasts.

1450 Wind gauge for measuring wind strength in use.

1593 Italian scientist Galileo Galilei invents thermometer.

1643 Italian Evangelista Torricelli invents barometer.

1752 Best tool Benjamin Franklin can come up with to study electricity and lightning is a kite, which he flies in a thunderstorm.

1844

The invention of the telegraph lets weather observers communicate with each other over long distances to track the movement of storms and spread storm warnings.

Circa 1915

Observations and measurements are taken from airplanes and with weather balloons using radio.

1920s

Radio broadcasts make it possible for the public to hear daily weather forecasts.

the Weather

1940s	1950s	1960s	Mid-1990s	The Future
Radar, first developed to spot bombers during World War II, is used to locate clouds and storms. **1946** Vincent Schaefer, an American scientist, performs first cloud-seeding experiments to produce rain artificially.	Weather reports become a staple of television news. Computers let meteorologists store and analyze large amounts of data.	**1960** NASA launches Tiros I, the first weather satellite. **1963** The United Nations forms the World Weather Watch to map daily weather around the world.	The National Weather Service begins using a network of 135 Doppler radar units, which detect hail, strong winds, and tornadoes.	Computers will provide forecasts 10 to 30 days in advance. Improved radar systems will locate dangerous weather conditions as they form. Advanced satellites will gather data in outer space, between Earth and the Sun, and monitor changes to Earth's atmosphere.

Activity

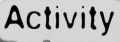

SURVIVING THE WEATHER Think of eight weather events we aren't able to change or control. Write what we can do to prepare for each one of them. Develop "survival kits" for four of the events, listing supplies you'd need to cope with the weather they bring.

WEATHER

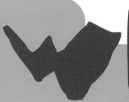

HAIL, HAIL!

Hailstones, hard chunks of ice, aren't always round. Some are elongated or jagged. They can be the size of gumballs, golf balls, and even baseballs. But the largest hailstone ever recorded in the United States landed in Aurora, Nebraska, in 2003. Measuring 18.75 inches (48 cm) around with a diameter of 7 inches (18 cm). Glad it didn't land on your head? Sometimes the weather can be a real pain in the neck.

Rain, Rain, Go Away!

It took centuries to figure out what caused a rainbow. If the Sun comes out while the air is still full of mist from a rain, its rays can be refracted, or split into the colors of the spectrum—red-orange-yellow-green-blue-violet (ROY G. BV)—as they hit the water droplets. Then the other side of the droplets reflect them back into an arc we call a rainbow. The rainbow appears in the part of the sky opposite the Sun, and only if the Sun is low enough in the sky. If conditions are just right, the rainbow may have a "shadow"—a double arc with the colors reversed (red on the inside, violet on the outside). Other places to look for refraction: in the spray from lawn sprinklers, waterfalls, and car washes. But a pot of gold? Forget it.

Planting a Few Seeds

Here is how, more or less, cloud seeding—making rain artificially—works:

- A plane drops crushed dry ice into a cloud.
- The dry ice attracts water droplets and ice crystals.
- The crystals get bigger and heavier until they fall to Earth.

The usefulness and fairness of cloud seeding is still debated today. Some people say it only slightly increases the rain that would have fallen anyway. They believe that making rain in one area steals rain from another. On another note, cloud seeding is also used to clear very cold fogs from airports. Now, is that debatable?

That Certain Glow

Tornadoes and lightning aren't the weirdest things to come out of the thunderstorm. Saint Elmo's fire is a faint glow occasionally seen during storms around protruding objects such as mountaintops, church spires, or airplane wings—even a person's head. Europeans once believed it was a sign of protection from a saint who kept watch over sailors during storms.

BRRRR!

When does 32° F (0° C) not feel like 32° F (0° C) but colder? When there's wind blowing. Those winter winds can make a cold day downright blustery, and the stronger the wind, the chillier it feels. Not surprisingly, this is known as the wind chill factor.

De-Lites

LIVING LIGHTNING ROD

Roy C. Sullivan was treated in the Waynesboro Hospital emergency room yesterday for stomach and chest burns received when he was struck by lightning while fishing.

Sullivan, a former park ranger, has been struck by lightning six times previously over the past thirty-five years. He has lost a toenail in a lightning strike and had his eyebrows burned off and his hair seared twice. He has suffered shoulder and leg burns and an ankle injury.

Sullivan is the only person known to be struck by lightning seven times. Lightning kills approximately 325 to 500 Americans each year, more than any other weather event except flash floods. Approximately 70 percent of those struck by lightning survive.

[Editor's note: Sullivan lived the final six years of his life without being struck again.]

'NO JOKE!

What did the weather do when it came to a mountain?

Climate!

How does sleet get around town?

By hailing a cab.

What did the rain say to the clouds when a hurricane hit?

I gotta blow out of here.

What's a tornado's favorite dance?

The twist.

Cultural Exchange

Hurricanes are almost unknown in Europe. In fact, there was no word for storms like these in English until Europeans settled in the Caribbean islands. The Spanish took the name of a storm god, Huracan, from Taino Indians. These storms are also known, when they occur in other oceans, as typhoons, cyclones, and severe cyclonic storms.

True? False? Or In Between?

1. Tornadoes strike the Los Angeles metropolitan area nearly twice as often as the Oklahoma City metropolitan area.

1. True. Environmental writer Mike Davis reports that the Los Angeles area is struck by a tornado, on average, every 2.2 years; Oklahoma City is hit every 4 years.

2. Alaska's highest recorded temperature is the same as Hawaii's.

2. True. Alaska's record was set in 1915; Hawaii's in 1931.

3. Nets are used to strain the water droplets from fog.

3. True. Scientists in Chile's desert have recovered up to 2,500 gallons (nearly 9,460 liters) per day by stringing these nets of fine nylon mesh in the path of blowing fog.

4. There is a town called Frostproof—and it really is!

4. Half true. The Florida town formerly called Lakemont is on a higher elevation than the surrounding land. That kept its temperature just above 32° F (0° C) during the big freeze of 1896, which devastated surrounding citrus orchards. Frostproof's citrus groves were spared. Residents petitioned to change the name in 1906. However, it's not impossible for Frostproof to freeze.

Final Project:
Green Thumb

Climatic events, such as the ozone hole over Antarctica or acid rain in North America, are caused by human contributions to the atmosphere.

When you and other people your age are Climatic events, such as the ozone hole over Antarctica or acid rain in North America, are caused by human contributions to the atmosphere.

When you and other people your age are in charge of the world, you will be making major decisions about Earth's climate. Here's a problem to start thinking about right now: global warming. It's called the greenhouse effect because it works similarly to the way a greenhouse lets in sunlight but doesn't let much heat escape. Gases that people have released into the atmosphere form a barrier that lets sunlight in but traps too much heat. The atmosphere lets in visible light, which is absorbed by Earth's surface, which then releases it back into the air as heat. The heat is then trapped and begins to build up. The more of these gases we have in the atmosphere, the more heat builds up near the surface of Earth.

Greenhouse gases come from an enormous range of activities and even from natural processes.

So what are you going to do about it? Gather friends and teammates around and:

1. Figure out the impact of melting ice from the polar ice caps. Study maps to learn where ocean currents will carry the water, and how that will change weather patterns. What areas are in danger of flooding? Of becoming deserts?

2. Study temperature maps. Which places will remain at comfortable temperatures after five degrees of global warming? Where do you think people will be moving in the future?

3. Research ways to prevent greenhouse gases from being released. What activities are causing the most harm? How can you convince people to stop doing those things? What kind of impact will that have on their lives?

4. How could you cool off Earth's atmosphere? Would it be smart to do so? Or will your actions have risky consequences?

ANSWERS

Solve-It-Yourself Mystery, pages 24–25:

You are in the Atacama Desert of Chile. Cold waters, known as the Peru current, swirl up from Antarctica past the coast of South America. Though the cold water is rich in fish and other sea life, they mean high-pressure air sitting in the southern Pacific that holds clouds far overhead. With low evaporation, the waters of the Peru current deliver very little moisture for clouds closer to the coast. Far off to the east are the towering Andes Mountains. Here the high clouds finally run into land and deposit rainfall. At the same time, the Andes block moist Atlantic air from moving west to reach the Atacama. So here by the ocean lies Earth's driest deserts.

If you keep walking another day, you will reach the city of Iquique (ee KEE kay), a port near the northern border of Chile, close to Peru. There you can catch a plane home.

Amazing But True, pages 16-17:

219 mile track/average speed 64 mph/3 hour, 25 minute duration.